MW01178087

TWENTY + CHANGE
NEXT GENERATION
EMERGING CANADIAN DESIGN PRACTICES

edited by
Heather Dubbeldam

Riverside Architectural Press

Twenty + Change: Next Generation

Editor: Heather Dubbeldam
Contributing Editor: Lola Sheppard
Design: Amanda Chong, Christine Kim
Production: Amanda Chong, Heather Dubbeldam,
Christine Kim, Joseph Villahermosa
Copy Editor: Doris Cowan
Publication Proofing: Leslie Jen

Printing by Astley Gilbert Limited, Toronto
This book was set in Slate Std and Univers LT Std.

Special thanks to the following individuals:

Our curatorial committee: Manon Asselin, Alex Bozikovic, Diogo Burnay,
Javier Campos, Sasa Radulovic

Our volunteers and advisors: Leslie Jen, Nancy Nguyen, Lola Sheppard

Those who helped make this book possible: Amanda Chong, Doris Cowan,
Christine Kim, Kevin McIntosh, Joseph Villahermosa

Special thanks to our Sponsors:
Canada Council for the Arts, Astley Gilbert Limited, Carpenters' Local 27,
General Contractors' Section, CRH Canada, The Dalton Company,
Royal Architectural Institute of Canada, Blackwell, KPMB Architects,
DIALOG, DTAH, Engineered Assemblies, Montgomery Sisam Architects,
Scott Torrance Landscape Architect

Canada Council **Conseil des Arts**
for the Arts **du Canada**

Published with the generous assistance of the Canada Council for the Arts.

ISBN:978-1-926724-73-7

Contents

Preface

Alex Bozikovic

As a design evolves, the rhythm of change is hard to predict: an idea can transform completely from one iteration to the next, or be whittled slowly towards its final state. Canada's architectural culture, in 2015, shows signs of doing both. As the curatorial committee for Twenty + Change: Next Generation examined more than 160 submissions for this exhibition, we observed two approaches to the 'change' that this exhibition embodies. Familiar forms and approaches are being refined by some of the country's emerging firms, while others pursue radical approaches to architecture and to practice.

The first group is reflecting upon the Canadian vernacular and the country's regional expressions of Modernism while achieving a high level of craft and an engagement with the realities of building. Its practitioners include Vancouver's Scott & Scott. Their home studio, which they constructed in part themselves, is an elegantly proportioned essay in wood, steel and leather. It speaks eloquently of the pleasure that architects take in building well—the resolution of details and assemblies, the poetic of materials. Their interior for the restaurant Bestie Currywurst also draws on this ethic, adding colour, flexibility and playfulness. A major element of this project is a grid of removeable wooden pegs, serving both ornamental and functional roles. This suggests just how much architecture can be achieved with modest means. The work of the Winnipeg office WORK/SHOP takes a similar route; their Fiskaoist outdoor dining area plays on the collective memory of a fishing hut, a traditional archetype, and creates a meaningful architectural experience of space and light—all using just lumber.

Another Winnipeg firm, Peter Sampson Architecture Studio, is similarly successful at building on an archetype with the Gillam Town Centre Railway Avenue Housing project. The jury appreciated the interpretation of a vernacular gabled form, tied to local history but transforming it into a form that is uncanny and yet evinces a 'can-do' attitude. Elsewhere, the office achieves formal and material innovation with its Assiniboine Park washrooms. That design employs shipping containers, not for their fashionable aesthetic qualities but for their availability and economy; after wrapping them in an elegant cladding of glass and wood, the studio sets up a compelling tension between reflectivity and opacity, the rough and the smooth.

In Sheshatshiu, Labrador, the St. John's-based office of Woodford/Sheppard pursues a similar aim with their Innu Aiamieutshuap church, which attempts to synthesize Christian religious architecture with traditional Innu forms; their Salvation Army Citadel is an ambitious, ephemeral update of vernacular church forms filtered through Late Modernism. Meanwhile, the Montreal-based office Microclimat strives for a similarly nuanced relationship to history with its La Taule Athletic Training Centre in Waterloo, Quebec; the form is a shed of almost iconic purity, while the material palette and exposed structure show great refinement. This is a thoughtful and robust composition, informed by history but striving for something relevant to contemporary life.

The exhibition also includes another group of architects who are moving further from what is expected of a Canadian practice, in approach and in design. UUfie's design for the Ports 1961 store in Shanghai embodies this ambition. The building uses one architectural unit, the glass block, to achieve multiple aims: it creates a building which is a spectacular object on the street and also evokes the vitrine, the essential element of a high-end retail store. This is a move of great elegance, combining structure, façade and expression of the program into one gesture.

Toronto-based Michaela McLeod and Nicholas Croft fully exploit the creative freedom that a pavilion—in this case at the Winter Stations event—can provide. Their HotBox is a pure form in the landscape: an elegantly proportioned black box, made unexpectedly of rubber—which, once inside, reduces the viewer's experience to facing up towards the sky.

Several firms in the exhibition are attempting to bring creative design to commercially driven projects. Batay-Csorba Architects, with their Double Duplex project, propose to reinvent the standard house typology of Toronto by going below grade and turning two house lots into four generous two-level units. Architects Luc Bouliane, meanwhile, achieve some spatial innovation within a real built project with their Relmar Houses, cutting away floor space to create atriums which provide a complex and rich experience as well as increased natural light. In the same city, Ja Architecture Studio took on a speculative project with the Offset House, combining their vision for a plastic, formally complex architecture with the realities of the marketplace. The result is something highly unusual in the city of Toronto. Meanwhile, their project Twofold, a mixed-use building, combines adaptive reuse and a familiar Canadian formal trope—the screen of slats—with an angular façade capped in brass. This relatively modest building, which houses the firm's own office, speaks assuredly of a new formal language and of a young practice's entrepreneurial ambition.

It has been eight years since the first Twenty + Change—a relatively short period in the glacial timeline of architecture—and the three previous installments of the exhibition have revealed a crop of architectural studios that continue to grow and change. The jury is pleased to see this new group of emerging firms, who are adding their own local contributions to the project of city-building across the country, and to the evolving project of Canadian architecture.

We offer congratulations to all of the firms included in Twenty + Change: Next Generation.

Curatorial Committee

Manon Asselin is a partner of Atelier TAG in Montreal, a multiple winner of competitions for a number of significant cultural and public commissions in Quebec. The firm has received numerous awards for design excellence, including three Governor General's Medals in Architecture in eight years, Awards of Excellence from the OAQ, the Institute of Design Montreal Award in Architecture, and several Canadian Architect awards. In 2008, Atelier TAG was awarded the Professional Prix de Rome in Architecture. In parallel to her practice, Manon teaches at the University of Montreal's School of Architecture.

Alex Bozikovic is the architecture critic for *The Globe and Mail*, writing about architecture, urbanism and related subjects. He is a National Magazine Award winner, and his work has appeared in other publications such as *Azure, Frame, Architectural Record, Dwell* and *Spacing*. He has contributed to books including *Concrete Toronto*, and he wrote the blog *No Mean City* from 2010 to 2014. He was educated at the University of Toronto and the City University of New York.

Diogo Burnay is an associate professor and the director of the School of Architecture at Dalhousie University in Halifax. He is a founding partner with Cristina Veríssimo of CVDB Arquitectos, an award-winning architecture practice in Lisbon, Portugal, and lives and works in both Halifax and Lisbon. Diogo has taught at Hong Kong University, Faculdade de Arquitectura University of Lisbon, the University of Minnesota and the University of Texas-Arlington, and is a visiting critic at schools of architecture worldwide.

Javier Campos, principal of Campos Studio in Vancouver, formerly a founding partner of Campos Leckie Studio, works along the West Coast from Baja, California to Haida Gwaii and has received numerous awards for his work. In collaboration with artist Elspeth Pratt, he has completed several large public art projects. Javier has spoken internationally, taught at the Isthmus School of Architecture in Panamá, and participates as a thesis advisor and guest critic at the schools of architecture at the University of British Columbia and the University of Toronto.

Sasa Radulovic is a founding partner of 5468796 Architecture in Winnipeg. The firm's work has been published in over 100 books and publications, and received numerous awards including a Governor General's Medal in Architecture, an Architectural Review Emerging Architecture Award, and several RAIC Awards of Excellence and Canadian Architect Awards. In 2012, 5468796 Architecture won the competition to curate Canada's entry for the Venice Architecture Biennale, and in 2013 they won the Professional Prix de Rome for their "Table for 12" project. Sasa makes design advocacy an ongoing pursuit through critical practice, professorships at the Universities of Manitoba and Toronto, and numerous public engagements.

Introduction

Heather Dubbeldam

Twenty + Change is an ongoing exhibition and publication series dedicated to promoting emerging designers working in architecture, landscape architecture and urban design. As the fourth edition of the series, *Next Generation* presents the concerns and approaches of emerging practices in Canada in 2015 represented by 13 emerging practices from Vancouver to St. John's. In selecting the practices and projects for inclusion in *Next Generation*, the curatorial committee found many commonalities in the preoccupations and design sensibilities of this cohort of emerging Canadian firms, many of which are highlighted in the preface by Alex Bozikovic and the essay by Steve DiPasquale. These included a strong focus on contextualism and the relationship to site, as well as the exploration of material craft, concerns common to Canadian architectural practice. From a group of over 160 submissions, the committee sought out projects and firms that displayed a level of invention or a degree of risk-taking—ones that stood out as pushing boundaries in program, design and tectonic explorations, or that offer an alternative approach to the practice of architecture. Many emerging firms have developed a more fluid relationship between design and construction, taking on the role of designer and builder. Some are also taking on the role of client, developing their own commissions in order to experiment with new ideas and expand the norms of what is available to the public for purchase or consumption. Many of these firms have overcome considerable obstacles such as restrictive budgets, conventional preconceptions or challenging sites and climates. Young firms are often more nimble, able to take greater risks and push experimentation, thereby expanding the boundaries of traditional architectural practice. In forging a different path than many of their predecessors, this generation of designers is exploring the potential for architecture to transform society.

For the purposes of this exhibition and publication series an 'emerging' firm is defined as one that has been practicing independently for less than 10 years, recognizing the long chrysalis phase of architecture, particularly in North America. It is worth mentioning that the majority of practices featured in *Next Generation* are less than five years old (more than half of them have only been in existence for two or three years). The firms included in this edition, with a few exceptions, collectively represent the youngest firms in the four iterations of Twenty + Change. Many of them have completed only one or two built commissions, or in some cases, the projects presented herein are their first built works. Other practices that have been around for six or eight years might equally be considered in their 'early days', as they refine their process, knowledge and craft. As a forum for celebrating young design talent in Canada, Twenty + Change also recognizes the courage it takes to launch an independent architectural practice. It is difficult to establish any business, especially one that is as fraught with the complexities and challenges that architecture presents.

Twenty + Change seeks to document and disseminate the thoughtful and innovative design work of emerging Canadian practices, recognizing design excellence, formal and tectonic innovation, and new models of practice. The national dialogue that it creates reflects current priorities in the profession and encourages discourse on contemporary architecture within the profession and with the public at large. Having been involved with this organization since 2007, first as a participant, then as a director, I have followed with interest the evolution of the emerging practices that were featured in past iterations of Twenty + Change. Many of the principals came from well-established Canadian practices, advancing the 'family tree' and language of Canadian design. A number of these firms have risen in prominence, grown their practices and are taking on larger commissions. Several have since received widespread attention for their work and are helping to redefine Canadian architecture. This forum offers an opportunity to both discover, and help promote, the newest and brightest design practices from across the country—the next generation of architects who may represent the prominent Canadian practices of the future.

Next Generation

Steve DiPasquale

In the coarsest anthropological terms, 'generation' is a convenient abstraction that helps us make sense of the various strata on the common kinship diagram—it denotes but one short stop in a litany of names tracing the family line. At its most fecund, however, the term sets off a complex narrative of just who these people are and why, of what ideologies, inventions, icons have shaped their particular perspectives. Understood in the latter sense, the 'next generation' show themselves most meaningfully not as the predictable genetic outcome of a pair-bond, but in their capacity to imagine opportunities for change that their forbears might overlook.

Like its predecessors, this edition of *Twenty + Change* presents a cross-section of contemporary Canadian design, asking this time that it be considered according to genealogical precepts. It is a collection of work that is as diverse in scale, typology and agenda as it is in the makeup of its authors—as such, it resists easy synopsis. But if there is anything that might unite the figures in this edition, it is the palpable drive to—if not make things completely anew—formulate new questions that cast the familiar in a deliberately strange light.

The designers of this generation find themselves, for instance, looking for ways to adapt to the pressing realities of urbanization amidst what French economist Thomas Piketty tells us is the new spectre of patrimonial capitalism. As the political lobby group Generation Squeeze succinctly puts it, younger Canadians are "studying and working more—to have less." A contingent of architects featured here have thus responded with projects that simply attempt to make more from less, to extract untapped spatial resources from existing sites. In Vancouver, Marianne Amodio Architecture Studio renovates a former seniors' residence, recasting a 150-square-foot bedroom as an apartment, and 10,150 square feet of shared amenities as a house; elsewhere in the city, they recalibrate the square footage of a single-family home to accommodate the lives of three sets of adults in the same family. Luc Bouliane, Batay-Csorba Architects and Ja Architecture Studio reshuffle standard Toronto lots to yield new forms—and new forms of inhabitation. And Peter Sampson Architecture Studio harvests decommissioned shipping containers—the spent shells of global logistics—to resolve a budget shortfall that had grounded previous attempts to furnish a Winnipeg park with washroom facilities. These designers demonstrate for us an admirable architectural prudence within a regrettable—though hopefully not irreversible—economic climate.

Others in the collection remind us that architecture projects might also serve as sites of progressive political aims. We should count it as progress, for example, that the design process of Railway Avenue Housing included consultation with First Nations stakeholders, and that similar procedures are becoming commonplace in projects across the country. It must also be recognized that this is the generation who have managed to turn the eco-politics of food into everyday practice, evident in Atelier Barda's choice to dramatize our shrinking biodiversity. Their installation, at once grave and ironic, mobilizes delight as a means to sanctify disappearing vegetable varieties, and provoke lingering questions about our complacency in the face of species extinction.

There is yet another kind of politics at play in this edition, one that invokes both senses of 'generation' outlined above: the politics of place. Projects that are decidedly—even fiercely—local in their scope of concern and material practice affirm their position within a long genealogy of architectural inquiry, but nevertheless search for new protocols rather than adhere only to those inherited. Scott & Scott Architects, in the refurbishment of their home studio, find meaning in working with local wood from log to lumber, but when using a 19th-century recipe for a beeswax floor finish, have no reservations about swapping out the traditional solvent for Canadian whisky. And in a small restaurant in Vancouver's Chinatown, the pair also executes one of the most successful experiments in contemporary grassroots economies: the architects first design a system from utility-grade lumber that enables owners to literally build and update the space themselves, and then resolve to outfit it with light fixtures and stools crafted by local designers. Finally, WORK/SHOP and Quinlan Osborne parse the logics of vernacular forms to make spaces of their own device. This group of architects, as Osborne reflects of his own relationship to the craft traditions he learned from his father, possesses the agility to "oscillate between old and new, between the understood and the unknown." There is, in their mental maps of their own practices, a kind of kinship diagram that allows them to proceed with intent.

This publication ought to be conceived in the same fashion—as a record that might help us understand our relation to the past and the future of design. This book, like the kinship diagram, is something to return to periodically, to see who and what yielded more offspring, to see which experiments turned out to be generative. We should hope that the work reaches any interested, but especially that it inspires the architects in every generation, those in whom the quest for private autonomy and public good happen to converge.

Twenty + Change: Next Generation Projects

Architects Luc Bouliane

Toronto, Ontario

Established in 2010, Architects
Luc Bouliane is a full-service design
studio located in Toronto specializing
in academic buildings, commercial
interiors and custom residences.
Founder Luc Bouliane, born and
raised in Northern Ontario on the
rocky shores of Lake Superior, often
looks to ideas of geology and nature
to conceptualize his work. Before
founding his own practice, he worked
with Teeple Architects, where he gained
essential insights into the art and
technical challenges of co-ordinating
a unique vision with a specific
architectural response.

The studio team's combined
experience as architects, interior
designers, and project managers
has broadened the office's ability to
complete a multitude of projects.
Whether creating a building from the
ground up or reimagining an existing
environment, the studio's strength
is in innovative spatial concepts and
material solutions.

Architects Luc Bouliane believes that in
a complex urban ecology, the buildings
that comprise our living cities,
neighbourhoods and campuses are
always interrelated. Each new structure
is an organism that must communicate
with its surroundings, advance a sense
of place and purpose, and integrate
sustainable building solutions while
simultaneously projecting a unique
character and beauty. The practice is
committed to exploring the cultural
understanding of space, community
and context as expressed in the
built environment.

The Relmar House(s)
Toronto, Ontario

Just to the east of the Cedarvale Ravine in Toronto, two semi-detached dwellings have been inserted into a narrow lot formerly occupied by a single-family home. The Relmar Houses are two halves of a complex organism, responding to two different sets of priorities. One of the dwellings is an articulated space designed to meet the nuanced requirements of a couple's dream retirement home. The other, intended for sale on completion of construction, supports the developer's strategic financial plan and is a fusion of spatial complexity and economic simplicity.

From the exterior, the project as a whole possesses an air of weight and dignity. Its brick and concrete exterior is divided in two by a vein of natural Algonquin stone; these strong, earthy materials give way to interior spaces of lightness and illumination. Access to daylight is limited by large buildings on each side, so windows had to be positioned tactically in response to the density of the development and its close proximity to site boundaries.

The cranked angles of the building are designed to capture as much natural light and ventilation as possible. A 20-foot skylight installed over an open atrium is angled at 21 degrees for maximum exposure to sunlight. The interior stairs below are shifted off the wall to allow more light penetration into the three-storey atrium space, and to reflect sunlight off the limestone-clad wall. The southern wall of the west-facing balcony is angled to allow better exposure to late-day sun. Bright tiles and glazed screens create interior environments that are both detailed and radiant.

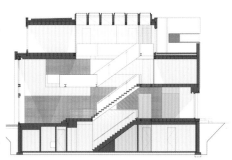

1   The exterior stone massing of the southwest corner
2   Private, fully landscaped rear courtyards
3   East-west section through atrium looking south
4   Floating office, pulled away from atrium wall
5   Light-reflecting glass and limestone in the atrium
6   Main stair and bridge opening to atrium above
7   Rear elevation opening to yard and green roofs

Architects Luc Bouliane

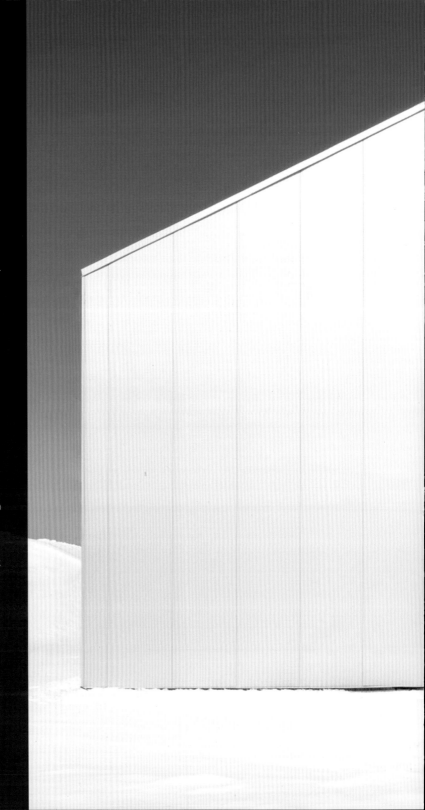

Architecture Microclimat

Montreal, Quebec

Architecture Microclimat is an emerging firm that was founded in 2012, currently managed by Guillaume Marcoux and Olivier Lajeunesse-Travers, both graduates of Laval University and members of the OAQ. Their vision is grounded in the principle that architecture and the environment in which it evolves are interdependent, perpetually responding to one another in a continuing conversation.

One of the greatest strengths of the practice is that it is a construction firm as well as an architecture and design studio. Consequently, the team's knowledge of construction enables them to take an idea from the embryonic planning stage to delivery, ensuring continuity and cohesion, and facilitating the exchanges between all the collaborators throughout the process.

Through the exploration of "microdevelopment," a concept that can be reflected in an area as small as a backyard, Microclimat seeks to realize the full potential of underused city spaces by rethinking them as liveable and adapted to urban life. This outlook offers city dwellers alternatives to traditional residences, and provides long-term architectural innovation that is adapted to its context.

Until recently, the firm's experience was primarily in residential projects, but Architecture Microclimat has now expanded into commercial architecture, bringing together under one roof all of the expertise required for a wide range of projects, be they residential, commercial or public.

LA TAULE
CENTRE D'ENTRAÎNEMENT ATHLÉTIQUE

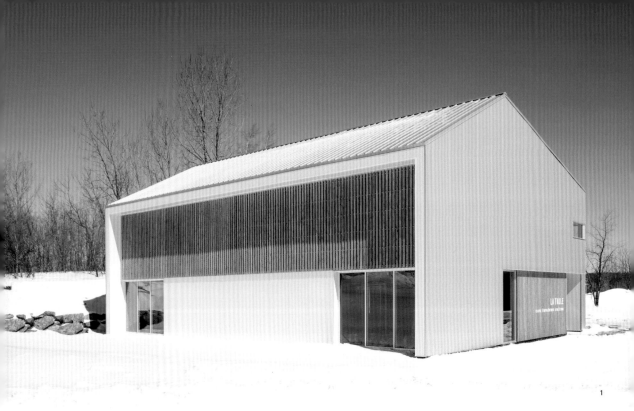

La Taule Athletic and Training Centre
Waterloo, Quebec

Located at the junction of Boulevard Western and Domaine de la Champignonnière in Waterloo, Quebec, La Taule Athletic and Training Centre is a lively hub of sports and cultural activities in a growing area of the city. The owners' specific goals for the 4,200-square-foot project were to share and promote a contemporary vision for a sports and physical training centre.

On the exterior façade, zones of vertical wooden slats create visual interest, contrasting with the pale grey metal cladding of the rest of the building. In the interior, exposed steel structural elements add to the impression of solidity and strength, and built-in equipment storage systems make efficient use of the walls. A compact but flexible and open configuration on the ground floor and the mezzanine allows for easy interactions between the different areas of the centre, and accommodates a wide range of athletic activities and community interests, from aerial silks and large rings for gymnasts, to facilities for Ironman triathlon training. In the summer, the large sliding glass doors open onto an outdoor training area with an elliptical indoor-outdoor track.

The positive effect of a limited construction budget was that the building size was limited, resulting in a larger area on the exterior for outdoor activities, thereby revitalizing a public space in this new residential city district.

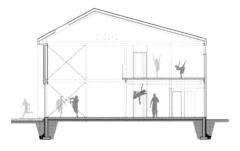

1   Training centre and exterior training space in winter
2   Building section: training space with mezzanine
3   Exposed steel structural elements and wood feature wall
4   Stairs and training steps to mezzanine
5   Gymnast in suspension in the double-height space

Architecture Microclimat

Atelier Barda
Montreal, Quebec

Founded in 2007 as an architecture collective by Cécile Combelle, Antonio Di Bacco and Julien Pinard, Atelier Barda studies contemporary regional transformations and seeks innovative and human-scaled solutions adapted to particular users and locations. Working from bases in Paris and Montreal, the team draws its strength from its cross-cultural vision and multidisciplinary practice.

Starting from an examination and understanding of existing elements, the firm's team members stimulate a dialogue and interactive design process for each project. This approach creates opportunities to develop strategies of minimal intervention that reinforce the project objectives while aligning with budgets and market constraints. The practice always strives to find imaginative solutions that resonate with the project's particular context. An understanding of contemporary urban issues and cultural attitudes is fundamental to all of the firm's work.

Atelier Barda advocates environmental sustainability in their approach to projects and a methodology supported by firsthand exposure to each context. Since its inception, Atelier Barda has been recognized for its originality and creativity in projects and competitions ranging from installations to urban spaces. With teamwork based on shared referents and effective collaboration, the studio is able to focus as productively on construction as on experimentation.

Chalet Forestier
Frelighsburg, Quebec

When Atelier Barda's clients decided to build a secondary residence near Montreal for weekends and holidays, they chose a woodland site on the eastern face of Mount Pinnacle in Quebec's Eastern Townships. Their requirements were modest: they wanted an easy-to-maintain chalet, largely open to surrounding nature, built from cross-laminated timber (CLT) to project a rugged and robust image.

The form of Chalet Forestier outlines a large volume composed of three programmatic spaces: parent/living, loggia and children's areas. The plan requires residents to go outside even in winter in order to move from one space to another, an arrangement the clients approved, feeling that it would bring them closer to nature. The loggia, extending between the two covered entrances to the living spaces, provides a screened exterior eating area, and allows access to the eastern exterior corridor whose composed colonnade recalls the trees of the forest.

Formally, the project presents itself as a large monolithic form placed on site in a dramatic manner. Far from blending in with the landscape, the black mass contrasts with the surrounding nature while creating effects of light and shadow that vary depending on the angle from which the chalet is approached.

1   View of chalet from approach
2   Plan view of study model
3   Exterior dining area
4   Living area
5   Wall-to-wall bookcase
6   Interior/exterior dining area
7   Master bedroom
8   Storage wall of firewood
9   View of fireside

Atelier Barda

5

6

Atelier Barda

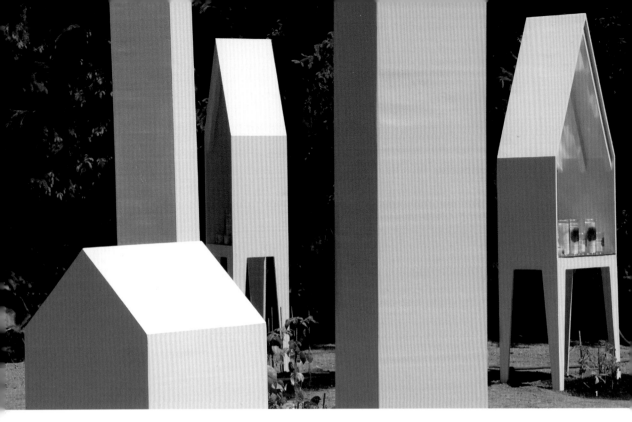

Sacré Potager

Grand Métis, Quebec

Sacré Potager (literally, "sacred vegetable garden") was an installation exhibited in Grand-Métis, Quebec, for the International Garden Festival during the summers of 2013, 2014 and 2015. The garden evokes the spiritual value of plants and their special place in our world. For millennia, people have raised monuments as acts of worship, honouring the sacred in both nature and human life. This garden is such a monument, created as a series of simple, elegant wooden oratories that recall the roadside crosses that once dotted the Quebec countryside. Within each oratory and growing in the soil beneath are rare native vegetables such as wild garlic, or heritage varieties that are no longer cultivated by modern agriculture, such as the yellow bush beans grown by early French settlers. The processes of production and marketing have divided us from the plants that sustain our lives. This installation gives visitors a chance to explore our horticultural heritage and appreciate the plants and the biodiversity they represent. It can be read on several levels: educational, nutritional, medicinal and decorative; it is at once a place of enchantment and an opportunity to awaken the conscience of the viewer.

Each of the 18 small chapel-like structures is dedicated to a rare forgotten vegetable. The varieties were chosen in collaboration with Seeds of Diversity, an organization that collects and distributes heritage seeds. Lit votive candles glow within each chapel, illuminating a hand-drawn illustration; a text attached to each candle describes the rich history and heritage of the plant. Intended to raise awareness and promote biodiversity, the garden also calls on viewers to make an offering to Seeds of Diversity, to help return these ancient species to our gardens and grocery shelves.

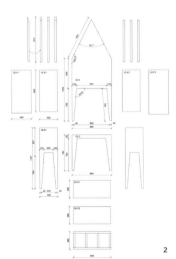

1   Garden of oratories
2   Technical drawings of oratory
3   Close-up view of votive candles
4   Oratories with gardeners
5   Close-up view of interior of oratory
6   Garden of oratories by night

Atelier Barda

Batay-Csorba Architects

Toronto, Ontario

Batay-Csorba Architects was established in 2010 by Andrew and Jodi Batay-Csorba as a research and development design studio in Los Angeles, California. The practice then moved to Toronto, bringing its open and innovative design sensibility to Canada. Before founding the studio, Jodi and Andrew had designed, directed and managed international projects in 38 cities and 11 countries, some on their own and others at Pritzker Prize-winning offices. Their work ranges from small-scale installations, graphic visualization and multi-media design to architectural and interior design and large-scale urban planning.

The partners' approach to a project begins by questioning standard building typologies in search of effective alternative design strategies. Batay-Csorba Architects base their work on the principle that architecture has a fundamental role in shaping how we experience the world, and that new ideas for interaction between the built environment and its users can create positive societal change. Since moving to Toronto, the firm has engaged in a number of built and speculative low-rise housing projects that challenge the standard domestic construction model and offer alternatives for social and public spaces in urban contexts.

Awards and recognition for Batay-Csorba Architects include an OAA Concept Award in 2014, participation in the 2012 Venice Biennale *Migrating Landscapes* exhibition, an AIA LA 2x8 Award (Los Angeles), an appearance as guest lecturers at the 2012 Festival Abierto in Panama City, and participation in the 2013-2014 *Protéiforme Architecture Paramétrique* exhibition in Montreal and Quebec City.

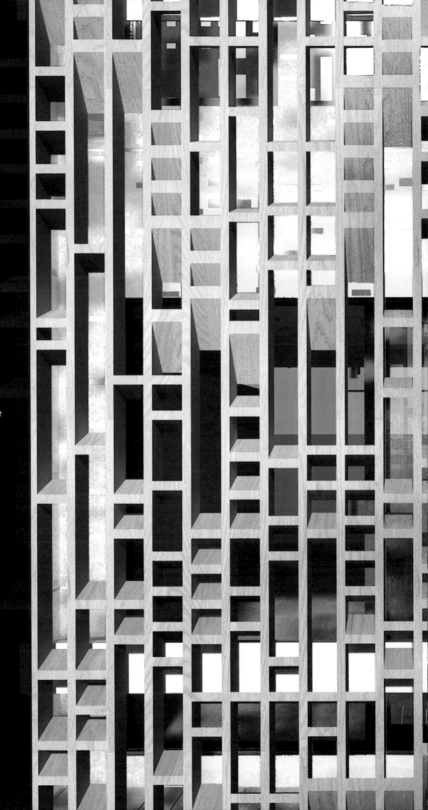

Core Modern Homes
Toronto, Ontario

Core Modern Homes is a seven-unit townhouse development that explores the potential of apertures to create visual interest while maximizing programmatic potential within an efficient volume. The design comprises two separate townhouse structures with units fronting onto perpendicular streets. The two buildings are clad in dark masonry, one in black and one in grey, to break up the overall massing and relate contextually to the residential scale of the setting. The variously oriented windows on the street-facing façades reference an inverted model of the traditional bay window found in much of the city's Victorian housing stock; their recessed and angled design contrasts with the monolithic effect of the masonry surfaces. Inside the residences, the window design maximizes natural light and ventilation, and extends views from the residences, establishing continually unfolding relationships between the interior, the exterior private garden spaces, and the sky beyond.

Designed with contemporary family life in mind, each of the seven residences offers generously proportioned living and dining rooms, a spacious kitchen intended for the active cook, and three bedrooms, including a serene master suite that occupies an entire level. Each unit also has a flexible loft space and a private exterior rooftop terrace. In addition, each

residence has a large protected outdoor living space resembling an internal courtyard. These exterior spaces are arranged to avoid overlapping views between units, enhancing the sense of privacy and separation.

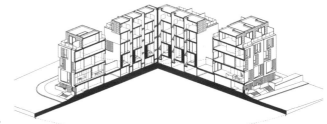

1 Entry view of Eglinton Avenue façade
2 Sectional axonometric of project
3 Perspective of Eglinton Avenue units
4 Elevation of Walder Avenue units
5 View of main floor

Batay-Csorba Architects

Double Duplex
Toronto, Ontario

The Double Duplex speculative development represents strategies for dynamic integration of exterior and interior spaces within a typical narrow and deep Toronto infill lot. An existing double-wide site was severed into two separate properties, and a four-storey 3,500-square-foot detached duplex residence was constructed on each site. Located in Parkdale, a historic neighbourhood of Victorian mansions, the project pays tribute to the beauty and artistry of the century-old architectural context through massing and geometry, using the register of the adjacent buildings' window and door heights, roof slopes and eaves to create an abstraction of bay-and-gable design.

Each lower unit is carved out in the front and back with double-height volumes that maximize natural daylight, flowing out to sunken courtyards wrapped in brightly painted murals by local artists. The upper units are organized around a two-storey atrium space with a large master bedroom terrace at the rear.

Creating a spirited urban design for the busy residential street was of key importance. Digital fabrication techniques and new material technologies allowed the architects to translate the perceptual and spatial exterior effect of 19th-century craft in the form of a two-storey brise-soleil screen, enclosing front and rear balconies and allowing controlled lighting and privacy inside the residences. Constructed of a bio-enhanced, rot-resistant and sustainable softwood, the brise-soleil creates a sizeable textural façade, referencing a large-scale art installation and angled so that passersby see multiple changing images; at night, the screen reads as a decorative glowing lantern.

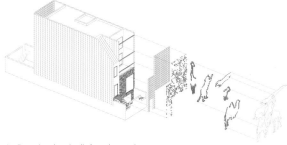

1 Front elevation: detail of exterior wood screens
2 Assembly drawing of front façade
3 View of interior second-floor library
4 View from above of the exterior front terrace
5 Perspective of front façades

Batay-Csorba Architects

3

4

Ja Architecture Studio

Toronto, Ontario

Ja Architecture Studio is a Toronto-based architecture firm with a strong interest in the role that design-oriented practices can play in bringing vigour to the development of cities. The commitment of the firm is to engage with ambitious projects that are both buildable and have cultural relevance. Founded by Nima Javidi, a registered architect, and Behnaz Assadi, a landscape designer, the studio was later joined by urban designer Hanieh Rezaei. Ja Architecture has participated in a range of successfully realized projects of different scales and has been featured in numerous international publications.

The focus of the practice is on finding ways in which form and geometry can inform each project. Whether it is the three staggered boxes of the Offset House, the oblique geometry of the Queen Street façade, or the roof of the Bauhaus Museum, geometric form has the power to create unique moments of tangency between a formal approach and functional necessity. The firm is interested in exploring geometry in interaction with natural light, a site's zoning constraints and existing boundaries.

Engaging in realized projects as well as speculative ones, the firm seeks to pursue a practical approach while keeping an eye on the future of progressive architecture around the world.

The Offset House
Toronto, Ontario

The architectural goal of the Offset House project was to capture southern light in a narrow and deep infill house on an east-west lot by splitting and offsetting the second floor. In section, the offset between the two levels becomes an opening that allows south light into the main floor; in plan it creates a space large enough for a straight cascading stair to pass through. In the elevation, the offset of two one-and-a-half-storey volumes on one hand defines the entry and on the other creates distance between the south face of the top volume and the house's immediate neighbour. Two intimate outdoor spaces are created on the lower second floor as the result of this volumetric shift. The geometric strategy was a manipulation of building form to create a house that constantly changes mood and character with the changing qualities of light during the day.

The windows, doors and louvred sunscreens are made of Douglas fir to contrast with the two white plastered volumes. The interior and exterior details have been simplified to give the spatial and volumetric aspects of the house more presence.

The project is a test-case investment by two companies to offer the public an alternative to the historicist houses that dominate the new home market of Toronto, and to challenge the idea that modern homes are necessarily custom projects for the cultural elite. This infill house is presented as an option to buyers looking for a new home within the average price range of the neighbourhood. The argument is that a house filled with light, even with simple details and finishes, outweighs the appeal of a house that imitates an old residential typology with expensive new products and materials.

Ja Architecture Studio

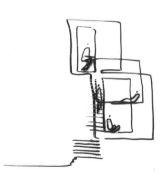

3

1   Front elevation on street
2   Offset House in the context of the street
3   Conceptual sketch of the two offset boxes
4   Interior view of the living/dining area
5   View of the stair and skylights from the upper floor
6   View of the stair and skylights from below

The Twofold

Toronto, Ontario

Located in a neighbourhood in transition on Queen Street West in Toronto, the Twofold is a renovation project that reimagines an existing three-storey storefront structure for multiple uses: it is a store, a residential unit, an office space and an outdoor gallery for local artists to display their work. The project utilizes areas of the property previously unoccupied by the original building, expanding into these infill spaces along both the main and west façades.

The design required careful study in order to successfully add to the dynamic textures already present on the façades of Queen Street. The new muntz (naval brass) cladding of the intervention contrasts with the appearance of the aged brick, marrying old and new. The flat-seam connection found in the roofing details of the neighbouring buildings of the same late 19th-century era was used to connect the panels. The original dormers of the building were transformed into two light shelves that use the reflectivity of the muntz panels to bounce light into the office interior, and are extended outward to act as oversized scuppers, leading rainwater collected in the recessed windows directly to the outside gutter.

The breezeway, with a tall brass-clad entrance on the west side of the building, has a twofold identity as both a covered outdoor gallery and an access route to the back bar entrance. The project takes an overlooked space and gives it a renewed purpose and presence within the community.

1 Twofold in the context of the neighbourhood
2 Exploded axonometric drawing of the structural components of the building
3 Multifaceted storefront with muntz cladding
4 Interior view showing the metal-clad dormers
5 Breezeway gallery

Ja Architecture Studio

Marianne Amodio
Architecture Studio

Vancouver, British Columbia

Marianne Amodio Architecture Studio (MAAS) creates architecture that is uniquely bold, achieved in a concise and practical manner. An architect who "… magically transforms ordinary spaces and humble materials into places of poetic beauty," Amodio's aim through her projects is to delight and surprise, and ultimately to design joy.

The practice challenges everyday assumptions about architecture; the work strives to be novel and whimsical, occasionally proposing weirdness as a concept and upholding the inherent charm of uselessness. However, it is never pretentious, always honest, open and playful. The studio utilizes geometric form combined with the effects of light to create mood.

Focusing on design solutions that explore alternative types of home ownership and lifestyles, MAAS believes that through creative thinking, new living spaces and buildings that respect and enliven streetscapes can be realized that address current pressing issues of affordability and sustainability.

APT Living
Vancouver, British Columbia

The new owners of a 12-storey micro-unit building in Vancouver wanted to modernize and renovate the building, formerly a seniors' residence, to create a new kind of micro rental accommodation. Renamed APT, the building has residential units ranging from 150 to 300 square feet. The challenge of the project was to convince potential residents that living in a 150-square-foot space was desirable—or even possible. The arguments for compact units of this kind were affordability and responsiveness to environmental and community issues.

The key objective was to create a co-sharing community, and the owners understood that high-quality amenities were necessary. The lower and main floors comprise approximately 10,000 square feet. MAAS renovated these floors to include not only the typical workout and gym spaces, but also art studios and workshops, laundry rooms and much-needed storage space. There are also private lounges that can be booked by residents, and larger areas for communal gatherings, a TV lounge, ping-pong tables and free wifi everywhere. The idea at APT is that the entire building is your house. Your bedroom and private retreat may be only 150 square feet, but your house is over 10,000 square feet.

In contrast to the otherwise white exterior, the balcony soffits were painted in varying bright colours. Intended to add interest to the streetscape, this move also added an element of playfulness to the building, and ultimately whimsy and surprise.

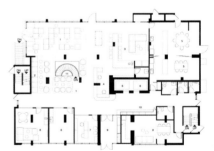

1   Colourful balcony soffits facing the street
2   Plan of the main-floor communal lounge spaces, including
    TV and art rooms
3   Main-floor lounge space at the communal coffee bar
4   Lower-floor activity space including ping pong tables

Marianne Amodio Architecture Studio

MAD(house)
Vancouver, British Columbia

The MAD(house) is a multi-adult dwelling in Vancouver. Housing three sets of adults from the same family within a 2,880-square-foot space, the design features large common areas open to all family members, and also separate private suites. Each suite has its own bathroom, bedroom and living space for residents to call their own. Small nooks in the public spaces also create a varied spatial experience within the contained footprint.

The house combines the contrasting aesthetic styles of the owners, one of whom is a strict Modernist and the other who prefers a more playful approach. Their shared love of Spanish architecture brings the design together and gives the home its delightful eccentricities: an exuberant use of coloured tile for the fireplace and other accents, a column that carries rainwater, and bright-hued glass terrazzo chips embedded in the concrete floor.

The planning of the space was an important aspect of the project. The design allows a maximum of natural light to enter, creating a sense of spaciousness, while full-height doors, soaring windows with discrete views at floor level, and wide-open roof decks add to this sense of openness. The private spaces in contrast emphasize respite and comfort. The MAD(house) provides a practical solution to multi-generational living while embracing a large family's whimsical and creative idea of home.

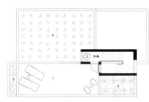

Marianne Amodio Architecture Studio

4

5

6

7

1   North (street) elevation with playful window design
2   Soffit at front entry with tiles representing the changing seasons
3   Floor plans
4   The main co-sharing space in the home with raised ceiling height
5   "Tunnel" designed as a transition from the entrance to co-shared space
6   Rear elevation with coloured soffits
7   Living room with windows placed to accentuate the height of the space
8   View of light and shadow through the screen and from under the open stair
9   Custom aluminum-grate guardrail detail
10 View of the stair with colour used to highlight geometries
11 Wood screen at the entrance with varying angled blades to reveal views slowly
12 Detail of wood screen with powder-coated metal base

Marianne Amodio Architecture Studio

Peter Sampson
Architecture Studio

Winnipeg, Manitoba

Based in Winnipeg, psastudio
is recognized for urban design,
architecture and building research.
Seeking to establish a dialogue on
environmentally low-impact and
socially rich places for living, the
practice sees architecture as an
investment in community identity.
The design team advocates for
healthy social ecologies, and
actively investigates new methods
of construction for low-cost
infrastructure in public facilities,
with a particular focus on the use
of reclaimed shipping containers.

The studio is a teaching environment
in which architects and interns work
together in an open studio to develop
ideas, projects and collaborative
decisions. In addition to private
residential and commercial clients,
psastudio's portfolio includes
public-sector work across Manitoba
with local school divisions, the
University of Winnipeg, Winnipeg
Harvest, and the Towns of Swan
River and Gillam. The practice is the
recent recipient of a RAIC National
Urban Design Award, an AZ People's
Choice Award, a Prairie Design
Award of Excellence, a Prairie Wood
Design Award, and a Canadian
Architect Award of Merit.

Assiniboine Park Washrooms
Winnipeg, Manitoba

Constructed from three decommissioned 40-foot-long sea containers, the Assiniboine Park Washrooms project makes use of these recycled material resources to overcome budget and construction constraints that were proving unsolveable through conventional methods. Each container houses a female, male and universal washroom. To maximize limited floor space, the containers are splayed to create two service cores. Each container is insulated from the outside through a secondary envelope designed to receive cedar siding. Inside, abuse-resistant drywall and tamper-proof fixtures—including recessed lighting troughs—have been installed, and each interior environment is enlivened by a colourful exposed container wall. To avoid seasonal flooding, the containers are raised and a wood ramp and deck conceals the resulting crawlspace while providing universal accessibility.

Built off-site, the washrooms went from concept to completion in five months. Because the containers are set on screw piles and borrow services from adjacent park facilities, they can be disconnected and decoupled as efficiently as they arrived, thus accommodating the ongoing infrastructural emergence of this prairie park.

The project is a programmed folly. The mirrored glass façade reflects passersby and the adjacent forest. Disappearing into their own reflections, the containers are three doors into the forest, playfully inviting users to come relieve themselves "in the bushes." When thousands of evening moviegoers meet on the lawn of the park's famous Lyric Theatre, the containers are an indispensable amenity. Glowing as evening falls, they become beacons in the night.

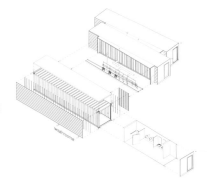

2

1 View west at dusk
2 Washroom assembly
3 Indoor prefabrication
4 Container doors for access to storage
5 Custom steel washroom signs
6 Containers being transported to site
7 Washroom containers on screw piles
8 View of washrooms and Lyric Theatre

Peter Sampson Architecture Studio

Railway Avenue Housing
Gillam, Manitoba

Gillam Town Centre is an 80,000-square-foot development that seeks to establish an urban core in advance of pending demographic and economic growth in Gillam, a small settlement south of Churchill, Manitoba, that is entering a phase of rapid expansion as a result of hydro-dam construction and road infrastructure work.

The first stage of the project, Railway Housing, is a main street complex that began construction in 2013. A new building block, with seven two-storey townhouse-style family suites and ground-floor commercial units below the residences, strengthens the mixed-use character of the downtown core. The design borrows from the durable and recognizable form of surrounding industrial buildings, and reinterprets simple elements to provide quality social and residential space geared towards attracting families and professionals to a northern environment. Looking for an architecture that would capture past and present while confronting a northern climate, psastudio in joint venture with Calnitsky Associates Architects turned the conventional public-private relationship upside down, so that living areas in the townhouses move upwards to improve access to low northern sun, while bedrooms are below, closer to the quiet nocturnal street life. Light wells bring ambient daylight into the residential suites. Inspired by the aurora borealis, bold colours in the wells add warmth to the interiors under the long winter skies.

Designed using the P.E.R.S.I.S.T. (pressure equalized rainscreen insulated structure technique) envelope assembly, the dual-barrier, double-insulated rain screen provides a very high level of air-leakage control that increases the efficiency of thermal management. This technical program was approved by the Manitoba Hydro steering committee, with the participation of long-term local residents and Fox Lake Cree Nation, to assist research into high-performance conventional building envelopes and provide a model for future construction in an emerging northern context.

2

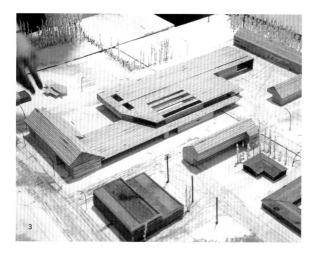

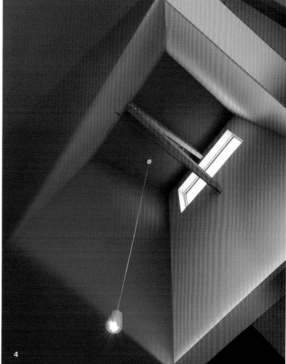

1   View of development along Railway Avenue
2   Building section
3   Master-plan model of the Town of Gillam
4   Light wells admitting ambient daylight into residential living spaces below
5   Two-storey townhouse-style family suites over commercial units at grade
6   Upper living space accessed by central stair below light well

Polymétis
Toronto, Ontario

Working at the intersection of architecture, landscape architecture and sculpture, Michaela MacLeod and Nicholas Croft are attuned to the natural and cultural influences that shape an environment, and approach each project with an interest in discovering how these forces may be constructed or controlled to reveal a familiar territory or space from an unusual perspective.

The studio's site-specific and sustainability-minded projects focus on making and experimental production with natural and synthetic materials. Technologies which blend manual and digital skills inspire new fields of exploration, which is the core of the studio's work ethos.

By investigating traditional techniques and typologies, the practice seeks to respond to each project with new ideas that are purposefully linked to both the site and its environs. The aim is to create works that are thoughtful, engaging and beautiful.

1

HotBox
Toronto, Ontario

An ice house (or darkhouse) is a traditional shelter used in northern climates for ice fishing on frozen lakes. In its simplest form, it is a temporary structure made of plastic tarps draped over two-by-fours. The building's purpose is not only to give basic protection from low temperatures and high winds, but also to provide a comfortable environment for what has become a social activity in many Canadian regions.

HotBox, created for Toronto's Winter Stations design competition, mimics this typology. The exterior is tall, black and cold; visitors pass through an entryway that blocks the wind and find themselves in a softly insulated, muffled and light-filled space that conjures feelings of shelter, intimacy and respite from the often harsh and unforgiving Canadian winter landscape. The contrast between outside and inside, exposure and protection, is heightened by visual, auditory, tactile and associative design elements.

The traditional ice house encloses a central opening in the ice. HotBox's opening is overhead: an oculus, lined with a mirror that reveals a solitary view of the sky, lets light and snow fall silently within. Like a winter coat, the skin of the hut is layered. The weatherproof outer layer is a thick, smooth rubber membrane draped from the top of the frame; the inner skin is fully lined with egg-crate foam padding. A single geometric form in a frozen landscape, HotBox conveys a sense of energy in a void. It renews its subject by reducing it to an abstraction, simplifying colour to an elemental contrast of black and white, and remaking a familiar experience in a new intensified form.

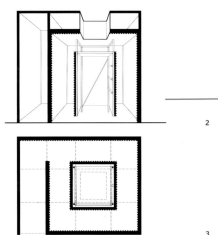

2

3

1   Exterior view looking west along Kew Beach
2   Sectional perspective
3   Plan
4   Exterior view of west elevation
5   View towards Lake Ontario from threshold
6   View through square oculus with mirrored reflections of the sky

Polymétis

4

5

6

Quinlan Osborne Design

Montreal, Quebec

Born in Ireland, Quinlan Osborne moved to Canada with his family in the early 1980s. He studied architecture at the University of Waterloo and initially practiced with architectural firms in Canada, the UK and Ireland. He cofounded atelier nu with Anik Mandalian in 2007, then established his own design practice in Montreal in 2013. His current focus is high-end furniture, limited-edition studio works and architectural projects. His work is held in private and public collections in Canada, the US and Europe, and has been published in magazines and periodicals both at home and abroad.

Growing up as the son of a cabinet-maker, Quinlan developed a strong sense of the relationship between design and the act of making. Understanding how something is traditionally constructed allows him to move between old and new, between the well-understood and the unknown, investigating the history and meaning behind a way of making before creating something new. This design methodology is an important aspect of all his projects, whether they are large-scale architectural works or single furniture pieces. He continues to find new and interesting ways to reinterpret the traditional in a contemporary manner, with an attention to detail and craftsmanship that he believes is too often lacking in modern design culture.

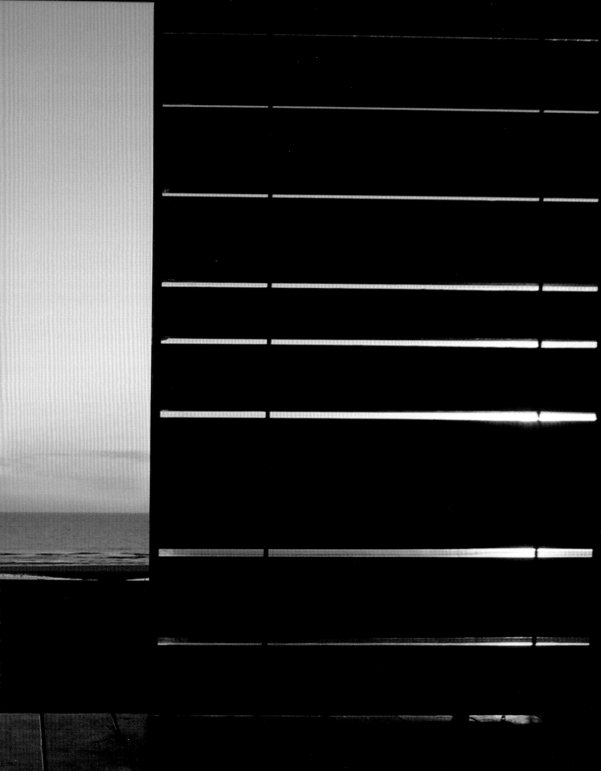

Beach Hut

Sutton-on-Sea, Lincolnshire, United Kingdom

The Lincolnshire region on England's east coast has a long tradition of beach huts, dating back to pre-war times; the older huts adjacent to the Beach Hut are reused WW1 bunkers. The project was commissioned as part of a larger regeneration scheme for the region's tourism industry. The design team's goal was a building that would echo the traditional vernacular beauty of the long row of existing huts on the site yet offer a contemporary alternative, relying on craftsmanship and meticulous detailing rather than a simple juxtaposition of contrasting forms.

The hut provides a cool retreat from hot summer weather, a shelter from rain, and a private changing room for swimmers. With no access to electricity on the site, the team decided to investigate ways of introducing natural light without the use of windows. Inspired by the way sunlight filters and flashes through the gaps in the siding of barns in the area, the designers aimed for a similar effect using red cedar and strips of transparent acrylic. Light passes through the edges of the acrylic strips, creating an environment of flickering shadows and a pattern of radiance filtering through the openings. The roof was treated the same way as the walls, allowing sunlight to enter throughout the day.

Glue techniques borrowed from traditional boat-building were used to incorporate the acrylic strips into a watertight single-skin membrane. The entire hut was constructed with traditional joinery tools; the roof and walls were made in a London-based millworker's shop as separate panels, then taken to the site where they were reinforced with stainless steel threaded rods and assembled by hand.

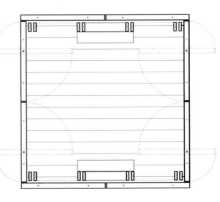

1   Side elevation of Beach Hut
2   Plan
3   View of beach houses in a row
4   Roof structure detail
5   Detail of acrylic banding

Quinlan Osborne Design

3

4

5

Scott & Scott Architects

Vancouver, British Columbia

After 12 years of practice at prominent Canadian architecture and design firms, Susan and David Scott built a street-level studio below their home off Main Street in Vancouver. The space includes a workshop for on-site production of industrial design elements, prototyping and material research. Their direct sourcing of local materials and re-examination of traditional approaches to material and construction have created an ongoing open dialogue with tradespeople, allowing the work to be designed and produced without a high degree of manufacture or heavy finish.

The couple established their own practice in 2012. They use design/build projects as a way of understanding the potential of materials and assemblies; this approach is central to their philosophy of building and design. They believe that innovation and refinement are born when the architect, working and reworking directly with the materials, has a collaborative role in the process of construction.

The practice's work has been featured in print and web publications worldwide, notably in books recently released by the art and architecture publishers Taschen, Gestalten Verlag, and Phaidon Press. In 2014, they were awarded an Architizer A+ Award for the design and construction of their Vancouver Island Alpine Cabin project, and also received special mention for the Bestie Currywurst restaurant. In 2015 their studio was an Architizer A+ Award finalist.

Bestie Currywurst
Vancouver, British Columbia

The Bestie Currywurst project was planned around the owners' desire to build the 25-seat restaurant themselves. Restaurateurs Clinton McDougall and Dane Brown, whose background is in art and design, wanted common materials that could be worked with a few simple tools, and a design based on a limited number of repeated everyday details. This strategy allowed the work to be completed on site with minimal shop support.

The project draws from the architects' and owners' shared love for matter-of-fact functional detailing, ad-hoc construction, and highly considered rational design. The work of fellow Vancouver designers, including Zoe Garred's Mariner lights and Joji Fukushima's bar stools, is highlighted throughout the space. The moveable furniture in the dining area allows for different arrangements to facilitate changing events. The kitchen is fitted with a hanging system for tools, steins and glassware that can be adjusted and added to over time. The main studio wall, an array of 116 holes and wooden pegs, is both display case and storage area, supporting an ever-changing rotating composition of locally produced art and design objects, coats, umbrellas, extra stools and pendant lights.

As with the stripped-down and simple menu of German street food made with locally sourced ingredients, the space celebrates ordinary materials and simple details. The tables and benches are oiled economy-grade spruce lumber, the hardware and counters are copper, and the painted floor and walls of the eating hall provide an attractive and easily maintained backdrop. The playfulness of the pegboard, the contrast of white with the warmth of wood, and the adjustable lighting all contribute to an impression of a craftsmanlike economy of architectural means.

Scott & Scott Architects

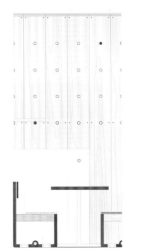

1   Kitchen wall with hanging copper and leather tool storage
2   Dining hall detail elevation
3   Dining hall
4   Close-up of kitchen hanging system
5   Dining hall with repositionable peg array
6   Bar

Scott & Scott Studio
Vancouver, British Columbia

A year after the launch of their practice, architects Susan and David Scott completed the refurbishment of the historic commercial space in their East Vancouver residence, a building constructed in 1911. The main space, once a butcher shop and then a long-running grocery store, has been stripped back to a simple volume lined with Douglas fir boards and completed with black-stained fir plywood millwork.

Using familiar local materials, the architects built the space themselves with a couple of carpenters. A sawyer on Vancouver Island, with whom they have worked for several years, supplied three carefully selected fir logs that were then milled and cut to suit the width and height of the space. The work was completed using traditional methods, while utilizing the availability of modern tooling. The south-facing storefront had been infilled by a previous owner, making it unsalvageable, but it was restored to an area of glass consistent with the original size using a single high-performance glazing unit.

The design is informed by the Scotts' desire to create work that is fundamental in its architecture and supportive of a variety of uses over time; they aimed to maximize the use of natural light, enhance the connection to the neighbourhood, use regional materials of known provenance, and acknowledge the lumber-based building culture of the Pacific Northwest. The interior fir boards are finished with a variation on a warm-applied 19th-century beeswax floor finish, its solvent replaced with Canadian whisky. The tables stand on blackened galvanized steel bases, with hand-stitched finished leather tops. Utilizing materials and approaches that wear and improve over time, they will also take on warmth with maintenance.

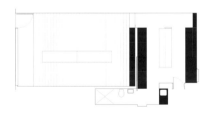

3

1   South window with heated concrete slab
2   Re-established street front
3   Section and plan
4   View from rear workshop to studio
5   Workshop
6   Studio

Scott & Scott Architects

UUfie
Toronto, Ontario

UUfie is an architecture and design studio based in Toronto, whose work spans the fields of art, architecture, landscape, furniture and product design. Established in Tokyo in 2009 by Irene Gardpoit and Eiri Ota, the practice moved to Canada in 2013, and focuses on design innovation that emphasizes the expressive qualities of space and materials. A constant theme is the idea of exploration; the team works at the centre of a network of skilled specialists, fabricators and craftsmen. Research into the context and constraints of each project is the starting point of the process, with a strong focus on the social and environmental integration of architecture and urban landscape design. The partners study multiple possibilities to find a design that will function with each project's scale, environment and site, simultaneously enhancing users' feelings of belonging, attachment and pride in the places they live, work and play.

The studio's designs have been featured in several contemporary exhibitions and galleries including the Design Exchange (Toronto, 2015), Salone del Mobile (Milan, 2014), and Guild Design Fair (Cape Town, 2014), and their architectural projects have earned numerous awards, notably a 2015 OAA Design Excellence Award for their Lake Cottage project, and a 2014 Project of the Year distinction (also for Lake Cottage) in the Best of Canada design competition. Current projects range in scale and type from private houses to major commercial and cultural projects in Europe, Asia and North America.

Lake Cottage
Kawartha Lakes, Ontario

The Lake Cottage is a two-storey, multi-use addition to a woodland family house in the Kawartha Lakes district. Oriented towards the lake, with a seven-metre-high façade, the steeply pitched A-frame structure is clad in black steel and charred cedar, creating a strong contrasting presence in winter against the snowy birch and spruce woods. The cottage design connects interior and exterior spaces, maintaining the ecological integrity of the site while choreographing an experience of living surrounded by trees.

The mirrored terrace reflects the forest, creating the illusion of a building floating among treetops, and provides a sheltered outdoor space that is close to nature in both summer and winter. The cottage has 14 openings to the outdoors, allowing cross-ventilation in all spaces. Light interiors are panelled in birch plywood and the detailing of windows and doorframes exposes the raw edges of wood, stone and metal. The staircase, made of a single log chiselled for treads, ascends to a loft space where an angled wall covered in stained cedar shingles reflects the sunlight coming from above. Deep skylights provide subdued light, and carefully positioned windows offer varying views of the sky, water and trees. A hearth offers warmth and a central place for residents to gather. These comforting but surprising elements underscore the theme of a constant, intimate connection with the natural surroundings.

2

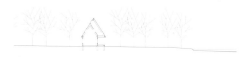

3

1   Exterior view
2   Detail of window
3   Site section
4   Interior view of living space
5   Reflection in mirror façade
6   View from terrace
7   Interior view of dining area
8   Interior view of upper loft
9   Exterior side view

9

Ports 1961
Shanghai, China

Located in a major high-end commercial district in Shanghai, the fashion house Ports 1961 wanted a new look for its flagship store. At night, the new façade evokes the idea of a glowing lantern, while in daylight it suggests a crystalline iceberg floating in the ocean of the city's constant movement. The structure seems to undulate, expand and contract as if responding to its environment, demonstrating the myriad possibilities of design experimentation, reshaping form, material and technology—yet at the same time bringing both traditional and contemporary interpretations into play.

The façade is composed of two types of glass blocks: a standard 300mm x 300mm glass block and a custom 300mm x 300mm x 300mm corner glass block. Unlike most glass block construction, it is not limited to a vertical plane. The combination and cantilevering of the two shapes of glass block create a sculpted three-dimensional façade. By incorporating innovative structural engineering and inventing a new joinery system in the block itself, the architects were able to achieve an elaborate and ornamental stepping canopy that naturally angles to the flow of pedestrian traffic, and allows the four bow windows to be visible from all directions.

The translucent glass block and shot-blasted stainless steel materials offer a serene contrast to the chaotic city. During the day, the façade subtly reflects sunlight; in the evening, when the surface is illuminated by embedded LED lights integrated into the joints of the masonry, the view is icy and sparkling.

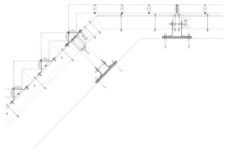

2

1   Exterior view
2   Plan detail of façade
3   Side elevation
4   Detail of entrance canopy
5   Night view

UUfie

Woodford/Sheppard Architecture

St. John's, Newfoundland

Woodford/Sheppard Architecture is a design and research practice based in St. John's, Newfoundland. Working on small and medium-scale projects throughout Newfoundland and Labrador, the studio creates buildings that respond to context and the experience of the natural landscape, balancing the demands of new industry in a resource-based economy with culturally and socially relevant design.

The studio group comprises individuals with a full range of knowledge and expertise in diverse fields including heritage architecture, art history, digital fabrication, sculpture, environmental sustainability and construction sciences. Completed projects include community centres, private residences, heritage restoration, adaptive reuse projects, and institutional park and recreational facilities.

Woodford/Sheppard's research engages deeply with the politics and availability of materials in an island economy, focusing on a continued investigation into the traditional uses of such local materials. The team is committed to using design and research as tools for the autonomous production of culture framed by context. They see this aspect of their work as a fundamental element of architectural practice.

Salvation Army Citadel

Triton, Newfoundland

The Salvation Army Citadel in Triton currently comprises a sanctuary and parish hall. It is located off a rural road connecting several small outport communities in Notre Dame Bay, Newfoundland and Labrador. The existing parish hall was no longer adequate to meet the needs of the church, as it was badly in need of repair, and building performance had become unsustainable. An addition was proposed for a new chapel, offices, kitchen, daycare and event storage areas to replace the hall. The challenge for the architects was to create a design for the addition that would connect to the sanctuary while complementing and enhancing the existing building and site.

The strategy for merging the new and old buildings was to create a wood-slat screen that would partially cover the existing structure and completely cover the new one. The screen varies in height and density, reaching up to 13 metres to create a new peak in front of the existing sanctuary.

The addition is placed close to the road to avoid further excavation of the steeply sloping hill behind the site. By maintaining the foundation footprint of the demolished hall, the addition's design allows the already excavated space to be transformed into a sheltered garden accessible from the lobby,

the daycare and the event space. The chapel, with a slightly lower tower, is the focal point of the new addition, while the office spaces and lobby act as a bridge between the two masses. The lobby bridge is glazed, inviting users of the church to enjoy the vistas in all seasons.

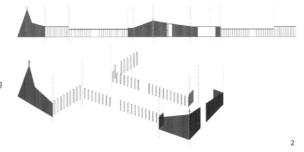

1 View of chapel entrance
2 Folding diagram of screen
3 View of front entrance
4 View of citadel at night

Woodford/Sheppard Architecture

Innu Aiamieutshuap 'Our Lady of the Snows'
Sheshatshiu, Labrador

Sheshatshiu is an Innu First Nations Community in the province of Newfoundland and Labrador, located on Lake Melville in Labrador. The community, having outgrown the existing Roman Catholic church, required a new building to accommodate larger attendance. Two types of gathering spaces were needed in the new church—one for large, less frequent events such as weddings, funerals and baptisms and another for small regular gatherings of the parish. The community wanted a non-hierarchical circular space for the small gatherings, incorporated within the more hierarchical arrangement of the traditional Catholic church interior. The round gathering area is located where the altar would traditionally be positioned, while the tabernacle, baptismal font and sacred sculptures are placed in the larger space. The lectern and pulpit separate the two spaces.

As a result of the church's remote context and the constraints of regional conditions, both exterior and interior are being constructed and finished with easily installed, locally available materials. Screens and decorative elements, such as window patterning and custom trimwork, will be designed and modelled in the studio, then digitally prefabricated off site. Similarly, the custom wood elements used in the heavy timber structure and the interior statues—representing the parish's patron saints St. Anne and St. Joachim—will be designed in studio and digitally fabricated. The courtyard is oriented towards Lake Melville, to allow activities to move outdoors, spilling out of the interior of the church into the surrounding landscape.

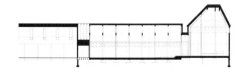

1   View of exterior and courtyard
2   Building sections
3   View of chapel
4   View of the nave looking towards the chapel

Woodford/Sheppard Architecture

WORK/SHOP
Winnipeg, Manitoba

WORK/SHOP, an architecture studio within a fabrication lab, is a dual-purpose studio for collaborative fabrication and research. Each project is an opportunity to discover different material methods and processes involved in the making of architecture. The practice was founded and is directed by Liane Veness, a registered architect who divides her time between teaching design and building technology at the University of Manitoba and leading the studio's architectural projects. The practice has won multiple design awards, and offers a unique approach to "handmade" architecture.

WORK/SHOP thinks and creates through building; the firm's team members all participate directly in construction and fabrication. Through their work, the office endeavours to resituate the architect in the role of the builder or maker who engages with the materiality of the process, and who relies on handcraftsmanship to connect design with materials and conceptual thinking with actual spatial experience. By taking part in this collective process, WORK/SHOP seeks to expand the traditional definition of the architecture profession.

Fiskaoist

Gimli, Manitoba

Inspired by traditional Icelandic fishing shacks (fiskaoist is Icelandic for "fish hut"), the architects used simple construction methods and materials to create an inviting outdoor seating area. The project occupies a very small space extending off the main pedestrian walkway of a street in Gimli, Manitoba; its design is a response to the town's rich Icelandic history and the traditional building methods of the local fishing community.

The challenge was to place a semi-covered structure on a site that was only 5 feet 8 inches wide and 23 feet deep, enclosed between two buildings and adjoining an existing patio. Because of these size constraints, a linear seating layout was the most efficient use of the narrow space. A custom-built bar counter running the entire length of the structure accommodates 12 people in a variety of seating options.

The walls and roof are clad with reclaimed 1" x 6" spruce boards, the floor is also reclaimed 2" x 6" spruce, and the 23-foot bar counter was constructed of laminated reclaimed fir beams, cut and planed down to size. The 1" x 6" boards used to envelop the structure are separated at the roof, allowing the sun to enter and create dappled light on the walls throughout the day while still mitigating the summer heat. Over time, the reclaimed spruce will age naturally, while the treated reclaimed Douglas fir counter will keep its original colour, providing contrast between the interior and the exterior of the structure.

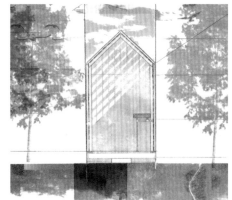

2

1   View from across the street
2   Hand drawing of building elevation
3   View from within looking out towards the street
4   View of the back
5   Hand drawing of building section

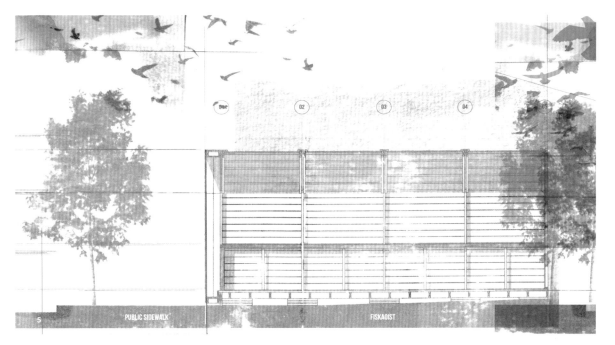

PUBLIC SIDEWALK   FISKADIST

Twenty + Change: Next Generation Project Credits

Project Credits

Architects Luc Bouliane
1259 Dundas Street West
Toronto, Ontario M6J 1X6
T 416 500 5927
www.architects-lucbouliane.com
studio@Arch-LB.com

The Relmar House(s)
Design Team: Luc Bouliane, Wes Wilson,
Natasha Lebel
Location: Toronto, Ontario
Completion: 2015
Construction: Mazenga Building Group
Structural: Blackwell Structural Engineers
Landscape: Fox Whyte Landscape
Architecture and Design
Photography: Bob Gundu

Architecture Microclimat
5179 Saint-Denis
Montreal, Quebec H2J 2M1
T 514 596 5888
www.microclimat.ca
info@microclimat.ca

La Taule Athletic and Training Centre
Design Team: Architecture Microclimat
Location: Waterloo, Quebec
Completion: 2014
Structural: Geniex Ingénierie/gestion
Construction: Construction et
Rénovation Devinci
Photography: Adrien Williams

Atelier Barda
5795 avenue de Gaspé, bureau 102
Montreal, Quebec H2S 2X3
T 514 360 2223
www.atelierbarda.com
contact@atelierbarda.com

Chalet Forestier
Design Team: Patrick Morand Architect,
Atelier Barda (Antonio Di Bacco, Kevin Botchar,
Lucia Font Bermejo), Lise Gagné Architect
Location: Frelighsburg, Quebec
Completion: 2013
Construction: Construction B. Lepitre
Structural: Innovation Routière Refcon Inc.
Photography: Atelier Barda,
Frédéric Bouchard, Yves Lefebvre

Sacré Potager
Design Team: Cécile Combelle, Antonio Di
Bacco, Julien Pinard, Patrick Morand, Ariane
Francescato, Lucia Font Bermejo, Théo Calvet
Location: Grand Métis, Quebec

Completion: 2013, exhibited 2013-15
Construction: Reford Gardens Team and
Atelier Barda
Researcher: Lyne Bellemare
Photography: Atelier Barda, Martin Bond

Batay-Csorba Architects
264 Jane Street
Toronto, Ontario M62 3Z2
T 416 524 2003
www.batay-csorba.com
info@batay-csorba.com

Core Modern Homes
Design Team: Jodi Batay-Csorba,
Andrew Batay-Csorba
Location: Toronto, Ontario
Completion: In progress
Construction: Mazenga Building Group
Renderings: Batay-Csorba Architects

Double Duplex
Design Team: Jodi Batay-Csorba,
Andrew Batay-Csorba, Lola Abraham
Location: Toronto, Ontario
Completion: In progress
Construction: The Mada Group
Renderings: Batay-Csorba Architects

Ja Architecture Studio
1070 Queen Street West, Third Floor
Toronto, Ontario M6J 1H8
T 416 594 2300
www.jastudioinc.com
info@jastudioinc.com

The Offset House
Design Team: Nima Javidi, Hanieh Rezaei,
Behnaz Assadi
Location: Toronto, Ontario
Completion: 2012
Structural: Blackwell Engineering
HVAC: Thomas Technical
Construction: Ja Architecture Studio
Photography: Sam Javanrouh, Behnaz Assadi,
Advirtour

The Twofold
Design Team: Nima Javidi, Hanieh Rezaei,
Behnaz Assadi
Location: Toronto, Ontario
Completion: 2013
Structural: Toronama Structural Engineer
Construction: Ja Architecture Studio
Photography: Sam Javanrouh, Mehrad Ahari,
Behnaz Assadi, Nima Javidi

Marianne Amodio Architecture Studio
127 East Pender Street, Unit C Ground Floor
Vancouver, British Columbia V6A 1T6
T 778 991 0155
www.maastudio.com
marianne@maastudio.com

APT Living
Design Team: Marianne Amodio, Stefan
Levasseur
Location: Vancouver, British Columbia
Completion: 2014
Construction: Eton West Construction
Structural: John Bryson and Partners
Structural Engineers
Photography: Ema Peter Photography

MAD(house)
Design Team: Marianne Amodio,
Stefan Levasseur
Location: Vancouver, British Columbia
Completion: 2014
Contractor: Novell Construction
Structural: Roger Wong
Landscape Designer: Beckie Stephens
Photography: Janis Nicolay

Peter Sampson Architecture Studio
707 Sara Avenue
Winnipeg, Manitoba R3G 0Y8
T 204 475 9323
www.psastudio.ca
studio@psastudio.ca

Assiniboine Park Washrooms
Design Team: Peter Sampson
Architecture Studio
Location: Winnipeg, Manitoba
Completion: 2013
Structural: Wolfrom Engineering Ltd.
Construction: Gardon Construction Ltd.
Photography: Mathew Piller, Elaine Stocki,
Carlos Schor

Railway Avenue Housing
Design Team: Peter Sampson Architecture
Studio & Calnitsky Associates Architects Inc.
Location: Gillam, Manitoba
Completion: 2014
Structural: Wolfrom Engineering Ltd.
Construction: Gardon Construction Ltd.
Photography: Mike Grandmaison, Carlos Schor

Polymétis
1947 Dundas Street West, Unit B6
Toronto, Ontario M6R 1W5
T 647 608 7347

www.polymetis.net
studio@polymetis.net

HotBox
Design Team: Michaela MacLeod,
Nicholas Croft
Location: Toronto, Ontario
Completion: 2015
Project Coordinator: Justin Ridgeway
Contractor: Zone Six Design Build Ltd.
Photography: Nicholas Croft,
Scott Norsworthy

Quinlan Osborne Design
770 A Bloomfield Avenue
Montreal, Quebec H2V 3S3
T 514 358 3498
www.quinlanosborne.com
studio@quinlanosborne.com

Beach Hut
Design Team: Quinlan Osborne,
Anik Mandalian
Location: Sutton-On-Sea, Lincolnshire, UK
Completion: 2008
Construction: Edvardo Aranovich Millwork,
London, UK
Photography: Atelier Nu

Scott & Scott Architects
299 East 19th Avenue
Vancouver, British Columbia V5V 1J3
T 604 737 2541
www.scottandscott.ca
hello@scottandscott.ca

Bestie Currywurst
Design Team: Susan and David Scott
Location: Vancouver, British Columbia
Completion: 2013
Construction: Clinton McDougall and
Dane Brown
Photography: Scott & Scott Architects

Scott & Scott Studio
Design Team: Susan and David Scott
Location: East Vancouver, British Columbia
Completion: 2013
Construction: Scott & Scott Architects
Photography: Scott & Scott Architects

UUfie
202-258 Wallace Avenue
Toronto, Ontario M6P 3M9
T 416 533 9999
www.uufie.com
info@uufie.com

Lake Cottage
Design Team: Eiri Ota, Irene Gardpoit
Location: Kawartha Lakes, Ontario
Completion: 2013
Construction: Level Design Build
Photography: Naho Kubota

Ports 1961
Design Team: Eiri Ota, Irene Gardpoit
Location: Shanghai, China
Completion: 2015
Structural: T/E/S/S atelier d'ingénierie
Construction: J. Gartner & Co. (HK) Ltd.
Photography: Shengliang Su

Woodford/Sheppard Architecture
11 Rowan Street
St. John's, Newfoundland A1B 2X2
T 709 753 7917
www.woodfordsheppard.com
info@woodfordsheppard.com

Salvation Army Citadel
Design Team: Taryn Sheppard,
Jessica Stanford, Chris Woodford
Location: Triton, Newfoundland
Completion: In progress
Photography: Woodford/Sheppard
Architecture

Innu Aiamieutshuap
'Our Lady of the Snows'
Design Team: Chris Woodford,
Taryn Sheppard, Jessica Stanford
Location: Sheshatshiu, Labrador
Completion: In progress
Photography: Woodford/Sheppard
Architecture

WORK/SHOP
82 George Avenue
Winnipeg, Manitoba R3B 0K1
T 204 296 2205
www.workshopprojects.ca
info@workshopprojects.ca

Fiskaoist
Design Team: Liane Veness,
Stephen Faust, Kyle Wires-Munro
Location: Gimli, Manitoba
Completion: 2013
Construction: WORK/SHOP
Renderings: Liane Veness, Kyle Wires-Munro
Photography: Liane Veness, Jacqueline Young,
Kyle Wires-Munro

Editors and Essay Author

Editor

Heather Dubbeldam is the principal of DUBBELDAM Architecture + Design in Toronto. Recipient of numerous awards for both design and practice, DUBBELDAM's work has garnered wide recognition in national and international publications. Heather is recognized as a leader and advocate for the profession: as co-director of Twenty + Change, promoting emerging architecture and design practices across Canada; as past chair of the Toronto Society of Architects; and as the vice-chair of the Design Industry Advisory Committee, a provincial cross-disciplinary design think tank and research group. She is the co-editor and author of several architecture and design publications, including the award-winning *Toronto Architecture Guide Map* and the four catalogues in the *Twenty + Change* series.

Contributing Editor

Lola Sheppard is an associate professor at the University of Waterloo School of Architecture. She is a founding partner at Lateral Office and co-editor of the journal *Bracket*. Lateral Office is a design research firm focusing on architecture's intersections with infrastructure, ecology and environment. The firm was the recipient of the 2012 RAIC Young Architects Award, the 2011 Holcim Award for Sustainable Construction for North America, the 2011 Emerging Voices Award, and the 2010 Prix de Rome from the Canada Council for the Arts. She is also co-editor, with Heather Dubbeldam, of the *Twenty + Change 01, 02* and *03* publications. She is currently pursuing research and design work on architecture, infrastructure and urbanism in Canada's far North.

Essay Author

Steve DiPasquale is an intern architect at HCMA Architecture + Design in Vancouver and the founder and principal of Operative Agency, a spatial-political research think tank. Together with Bryan Beça, he recently completed *The Space of Difference*, an interactive video installation commissioned by the Surrey Art Gallery. They also won the People's Choice Award for their submission to the Vancouver installment of the Migrating Landscapes exhibition. Steve has written several articles for *Canadian Architect* magazine, including reviews of the Monte Clark and Equinox galleries, and the Sechelt/Shíshálh Hospital.

Next Generation Sponsors

Twenty + Change would like to thank the following sponsors who
generously helped make this exhibition and publication possible.

Publication Sponsors
Canada Council for the Arts
Astley Gilbert Limited

Primary Sponsors
Carpenters' Local 27
General Contractors' Section Toronto
CRH Canada

Supporting Sponsors
The Dalton Company
Royal Architectural Institute of Canada
Blackwell Engineering
KPMB Architects

Exhibition Print Sponsor
Astley Gilbert Limited

Exhibition Sponsors
DIALOG
DTAH
Engineered Assemblies
Montgomery Sisam Architects
Scott Torrance Landscape Architect

Donations-in-Kind
Urbanspace Gallery

 Canada Council for the Arts   Conseil des Arts du Canada 

   DALTON *building on principles*

RAIC | IRAC Architecture Canada   **Blackwell**   **KPMB Architects**

 **DIALOG** **dtah** ENGINEERED ASSEMBLIES MontgomerySisam Scott TORRANCE LANDSCAPE ARCHITECT INC.